MOMENTS CALLED LIFE

A COLLECTION OF ALL THESE LITTLE MOMENTS PASSING BY...

UMRA

To my beloved sister, Aqsa, and my precious brother Mohd. Taha.

And to my family and friends, who together have made me who I am, and pieced together to complete the puzzle of my life. And my teachers who believed in me and supported me throughout this journey.

Contents

Contents

Contents

Contents

Preface

Our souls are entwined with the people we love and the people we love our entwined with words. "Moments Called Life," brings you the people you have lost and the people you have found in the congregation of these poetically arranged words. Feel the sensations and warmth of love seeping into your heart. Experience the thrills of feelings through the words I handpicked for you. I hope this book will surge emotions in you, which you thought you could never experience again. Let these words drown in the realm of emotion and give birth to a new human in you. Take this time to accept your emotions and be grateful for the things that happened and what they made you feel. On this expedition of acknowledgement and gratitude for your emotions, I hope you feel grateful for this book too.

Prologue

Moments Called Life is a capsule of moments, and emotions, we deny, repress, and fear. *Moments Called Life* brings all of those moments, and emotions, back to you. It is time for you to face them, and feel them, Let's take a pause and think about all the atrocities your soul went through just because you were ashamed of your emotions. Read this book and let yourself feel what you want to feel. Set yourself free, and let yourself find your way to you.

I hope you discover yourself in a new way at the end of this book. I hope it connects you to who you are and accept what you were. I hope you take something good out of this book.

Happy Reading!

1. Smile On My Face

I walk in each day,
With a smile on my face.
A facade to cover every tear's trace.
I fear that I'll lose—
But what I fear more is to let people know that I'm afraid.
My life has been tragedy's favourite muse,
In the garden of sorrow, I played.
I feel like I'm losing my sanity,
I'm afraid I'd long to be loved all eternity.
My breaths choke me,
My thoughts rip me apart.
My tears sting me,
I don't know how did it start,
Someday things will get better, I pray,
I walk in each day,
With a smile on my face.

I'm chained in my head,
Eyes wide open as I lay in my bed.
I want to tell you how my heart burns with every drop of my
tear,
But you'd hate me too, that's what I fear.

I want tell you how I'm losing my mind,
How these 'made up' monsters are so unkind.
But I fear you'd never want to see my face,
If I show you how much of a loser I am in this race.
So I walk in each day,
With a smile on my face.
My fears are driving me crazy,
My vision is all dull and hazy.
I am unable to pull myself out,
Nobody can hear me, while inside my head I shout.
I can't do it anymore,
I am drowning and can't find the shore.
I must be going insane,
But sometimes I think I am pulling all this for fame.
Who should trust me?
When even I don't trust myself.
Something's been killing me,
And maybe I'm murdering myself.
'It'll end,' I tell myself. 'It's just a phase,
So I walk in each day,
With a smile on my face.

My silent pleas call your name,
I suppress them to save myself from shame.
I'm trying…trying every day,
My skin singes like bare feet at noon in May.
But all that I do is 'not enough,'

The monsters in my head make me cry till my eyes puff.
They tell me, 'You hate me!'
They tell me you won't set me free.
I want to tell you how they hurt me every night and day,
'You don't care!' They say,
I'm afraid they're right, so I walk in each day,
With a smile on my face.

I want to press you tight against my burning heart,
But I don't want to be the reason you thwart.
I can't heal myself while you hurt,
So I bury myself in the depths of dirt.
I feel you just hear me as an obligation of sympathy,
You don't have to do that when I already know you don't love
me.
I spare you of the pain I bear,
My darling I'd kill myself to save your tears.
Your voice clears the mist of noise in my mind,
I thank you for being so patient and kind.
But I can't let you suffer while comfortable in your bed, you lay.
So I walk in each day,
With a smile on my face.

2. On A Starry Night

On a starry night,
Walking side by side,
Your hands entwined in mine,
Across our lips lingering irrepressible smiles.
That's my wildest dream,
To count stars while brighter our eyes gleam.
Though I am a little coy,
But let me tell you, I dedicate my whole life to bring you joy.
When the sky is a total sight,
All I wish is to have you with me to share the beauty of night,
Walking side by side.
Your hands entwined in mine,
Across our lips lingering irrepressible smiles.

To wake up and find you beside,
To have seen you a great number of times,
But still stare at you each morning with eyes open wide.
To share my coffee cups,
And read you my favourite books.
To make you smile,
When you can't even cry.
To kiss you good night,

And hold you when the day gets bright.
All I wish is to hold you tight,
On a stormy night.
Sitting side by side,
Your soul entwined in mine,
Across our hearts lingering the happiness of all our lifetime.

To snuggle with you when you catch a cold,
Get myself sick too when, 'I'll catch a cold' you warned.
To dance with you in mid-August's rain.
To collapse in your arms when I am drained.
To climb mountains with you,
And swim oceans too.
To tell you that I love you,
When you think even you can't love yourself too.
All I wish is when things get tight,
You find me right beside.
My arms ready for you to hide.
Across your soul lingering the warmth that'll make you feel alive.
On a starry night,
Walking side by side,
Your hands entwined in mine,
Across our lips lingering irrepressible smiles.

3. You And I

Just if you ever look me in the eye,
You'll be able to see a world consisting of only you and I.
There I shower you with love and care,
And ruffle your thick curly hair.
I press you to my heart,
And you faintly quiver in my arms,
As if out of the entire world I am your favourite nook,
As you snuggle in my arms I read to you, your favourite book.
We melt into each other as if the heavens are melting into the
lowest sky,
Just if you ever look me in the eye,
You'll be able to see a world consisting of only you and I.

There you don't sleep without kissing me goodnight,
There my morning starts with having you beside.
There we even pray together every day,
And bake chocolate cakes on Sundays.
You run to me when you want to feel safe,
My arms do not have to resist taking you in my embrace.
Where we share every laugh and every cry,
Just if you ever look me in the eye,
You'll be able to see a world consisting of only you and I.

Our little world smells of roses and pies
Just if you ever look me in the eye,
You'll be able to see a world consisting of only you and I.

There we dance and laugh in the living room,
We fight our way through the fumes.
And you teach me how to play that guitar,
And we laugh about our antics at the tea hour.
And when our hair turns greasy and grey,
We'll have lots of cats walking about our home all night and day.
We swim across oceans and fly through the sky,
Just if you ever look me in the eye,
You'll be able to see a world consisting of only you and I.

There when you get sick you don't drive me away,
On weekends like little children, we giggle and play.
And when your chest is heavy from the atrocities of life,
You sink your head in my lap and stay like that for a while.
I make you laugh and in my presence, you even feel safe enough
to cry,
Just if you ever look me in the eye,
You'll be able to see a world consisting of only you and I.

4. There'll Come A Day

And then there'll come a day you'll have to let go.
The dreary winters we spent,
Laughing with friends,
Painting the sombre canvasses,
With sanguine hopes of gold and brasses.
It all slips out of your hands as it flows,
And then, there'll come a day you'll have to let go.

The peals of laughter and pangs of sorrow,
The troubles, we had borrowed.
Slouching through heavy loads of mischief,
Who knew these days would be so brief?
It runs faster the more you wish for it to move slow,
And then, there'll come a day you'll have to let go.

At uncanny places, we'll roam,
When once the place we called ours will no longer be home.
Howling winds and reminiscent storms,
All over your mind memories will be taking a toll.
It might feel like a heavy blow,
But then, there'll come a day you'll have to let go.

UMRA

Faded remains of gilt bloom,
That'll be all you'll be left with during autumn gloom.
Deep somewhere in your heart your love wrapped in shrouds,
Miserably lonely when you'll pass through the crowds.
On your own then you'll learn to grow,
And then, there'll come a day you'll have to let go.

When the days were buoyant and bright,
Soon the dreams you had then sown will ripe,
It might be hard to swallow,
Your fruits might be insipid and hollow.
Let that not stop you from more seeds to sow,
And then, there'll be a day you'll have to let go.

Old paens might make you mourn,
In shreds, you might find your heart torn.
The hands you held onto so tight,
Will slip off someday, to your fright.
Life might make you feel like a bear in a circus show,
But there'll be a day you'll have to let go.

The fiends in your head might slit your mind,
But lest without giving a tough fight.
So you may be glorified with time,
And could be heard in the wind's chimes.
You're not made for past regrets and worries of tomorrow,
Thus, there'll be a day you'll have to let go.

There'll be days when you'll scream and weep,
Your heart will almost give in to the agony.
Scattered on the floor your soul's shards,
Felicity of youth buried in the graveyard.
But you can't run from it as you know,
And then, there'll be a day you'll have to let go.

5. The Man I Hate The Most

I hate all men,
But there's a man I hate the most,
For the way he makes me fall.
For the way he makes me fall for his mischievous smiles,
And little lies.
For the way he makes me want to love him,
When I can't hate him,
the way I hate most men,
Because I hate him the most,
For the way he has made me fall.

He makes me fall at his very sight,
He makes me fall for his eyes so bright.
He makes me fall for his loose wristwatch,
He makes me fall at his very thought.
He makes me fall for his name,
He beats me at my own game.
He makes me fall for his clumsy manners,
I hate the way we fight and yet I love all the banters.
Most of all I hate the way I hate him,

For I hate all men,
But I hate him the most,
For the way he makes me fall.

I hate the way he makes me smile,
When he isn't even trying.
I hate the way he makes me forget all the conduct,
I hate the way how in his soul he has mine tucked.
I hate the way I lose it when he gets a small scratch,
All those other men I see are not even a match.
I hate him with all of me, mostly because I love all of him,
Because I hate all men,
But I hate him the most,
For the way he makes me fall.

I hate him the most,
But I love him even more.
I love the way he makes me feel safe,
Cradling me in his arms when the city's ablaze.
I love the way he makes my parch heart bloom,
Pouring my cracks with generosity amidst doom.
I love the way he lets me grow,
He watered my soul when others ceased to my shade.
I love him but I hate him,
Because I don't want to fall.

I witness everyone getting love while I can't.

And that's why I hate all men,
But I hate him the most,
For every time I look at him,
He makes me want to fall.

6. Exquisite

He is like the flowing water of the holy lake,
Unsettled but serene.
He moves like the gusting wind,
Filling my heart with sensations, by a touch unseen.
His smile is like the crack of dawn,
Showering the world with a golden glow.
And don't even get me started on how his hair flutter,
When the winds blow.
His spirit so free and wild—
Like a fox dancing at the hilltop on a full moon.
His soul, so full of life,
Like the vibrant nights of mid-June.
He is in every beautiful thing I see,
Or is he the only thing I see?

He is in the snow-covered mountains,
He is in the aroma of moist soil when it rains.
He is in the sunset's orange and pink,
He is in my pen's ink.
He is in every beautiful thing I see,
Or is he the only thing I see?

7. When Love Blooms

The moment I laid my eyes on you—
I knew you were my favourite dream.
To colour the gloomy canvas of my life you were fate's scheme.
The day I found you standing in the rain—
I realised my life was a story and you were the theme.

For me, you were always more than enough.
For me, you were ease in the rough.
You became my safe place when times were tough.
Your pretty eyes made me bloom.
Your smile would take away my gloom.
The wind brushing through your hair—
would turn heads in every room.
How do I explain your beauty?
My darling, even your silhouette is enough to wreak doom.

When my eyes kiss your smile,
I'd stare at you for more than a while.
I wish to walk hand in hand with you for miles.
To drive me all crazy for you, my darling, you have lots of guiles.

I am unworthy of even holding you in my heart,

For you, my love! Are a living piece of art.
I am blessed to have you, my dear,
nothing compares to the bliss of having you near.
I never ask to be with you, but I want to be you,
So that whenever I look within myself I'll find you there.
The moment I laid my eyes on you, I knew you were my
favourite dream.
A gift by God, to teach me what love actually means.

8. Let's Not Give It A Name

Let's not give it a name,
Though his love has set my heart on flame,
Let's still not give it a name.

He brings spring to my life's late fall,
But let's not ponder upon what my feelings should be called.
It is surely not love,
But I conceal my agony just not to let him suffer,
So what is it if it's not love?
The more I run from him, I fall for him harder,
It's surely not love,
But what is it if it's not love?

Let's not think about what to call this,
And why do I care for him?
Whoever has his heart, my heart is his,
He has already been more than I asked for—
what more can I ask from Him?

Every time I thought of being away from him, my heart
pounded,
If I give it a name it will get bounded.
Let's not give it a name,
Though in my heart he has a claim.
It's a flight to heaven when we walk,
For the rest of my life, I can hear him talk.
I look for him everywhere,
But look down when he's there.
They can call it whatever they want,
He's my favourite part of this life's jaunt.
But I won't decide what it should be called,
Never going to tell him how my heart for him has longed.

I'll leave these unexpressed feelings nameless,
Naming something as pure as this—
with polluted words is aimless.
Giving names to loads of emotions is just lame,
So let's not give it a name…

9. Youth Spring

He has those pretty eyes,
And a pretty smile,
A funny nose,
And hands as soft as a rose.
But what I love about him is he's like a lime,
Lost in his own world as if he's a master of crime.
His voice as sweet as honey,
He's sometimes sour when he's trying to be funny.

The way he turns his head,
when I call his name.
He is so gentle like a flower bed,
Can't help my smile when he does something lame.
He never asks for help when things mess up,
He grows in the wild like a buttercup.
Yes, he can sometimes be crazy,
But he brings me warmth when it's hazy.

He's got his scent from gardens of springs,
Warmth and delight he carries everywhere with him.
He's got the glow of sun rays at the crack of dawn,
Withering my life when he's gone.

Serene like the moon,
His eyes tickling my soul wreak doom.

I love him as he is,
And don't care if he loves me.
But today I reveal my affections,
Because I love him more than one's heart can.
He's messy and his hair unkempt,
I try not to fall but fail at every attempt.
Loving him is not easy,
But not giving up is what love is, maybe.
He's the finest painting in the world's art hall,
He's the first spring of my youth and I couldn't help but fall.

10. Children of Earth

Longing to be loved are the children of Earth,
Carved out of blood and dirt.
Pale puppets sucked out of love,
Drenched in scarlet the ivory dove,
Scattered over the floor scarred souls and its shards,
Unseen like a ghoul and counting on a house of cards.
Wondering when they'll be 'enough,'
Crushing themselves into the grindstones and acting tough,
I've seen this play before,
Masking all the pain while you're shaking to the core.
Soaked in crimson and doused in hearth,
The epitome of grief are the children of earth,
Carved out of blood and dirt,
Suffer no more, Oh! Children of Earth.
Only the embrace of death can quench this dearth,
Fuel these fiery flames with all fears burning in your girth.
Made for some grotesque memories are the children of earth.

Stinging scars and bloodshot eyes,
None to hear their pleas and cries.
Smiling with a burning coal on their tongue,
Mist of fear filling their lungs.

Grasses of grief pricking their skin,
Rains of blood leaving them bleeding.
The fiery sky burning against their heart,
I've once seen this sort of art,
All those strokes tearing you apart.
Soaked in crimson and doused in hearth,
The epitome of grief are the children of earth,
Carved out of blood and dirt.
Suffer no more, Oh! Children of Earth.
Only the embrace of death can quench this dearth,
Fuel these fiery flames with all fears burning in your girth.
Made for some grotesque memories are the children of earth.

Who are these children and what were they made for?
Giving up every piece of them and yet unknown.
Who are these children and what was their fault?
Robbed out of their childhood and looted the love of their vaults.
Who are these children and what do they want?
An embrace that protects them from the memories that haunt.
Who are these children and where do they go?
They're a shade to scorching souls but have no place of their own.
Who are these children as pure as doves?
They're the omen of misfortune and vandals of love.
Carved out of nothingness,
Yearning to be emptied of this emptiness.
Soaked in crimson and doused in hearth,
Trying to be something are the children of Earth,

Carved out of blood and dirt,
Suffering to be something are the children of Earth.
Only the embrace of death can quench their dearth,
Fuelling the fiery flames with all fears burning in their girth.
Made for some grotesque memories are the children of earth.
Longing for love are the children of the Earth.
Longing for love are the children of the Earth.

11. Serendipity

You were the most beautiful thing that ever happened to me,
The way our hands brushed,
The way I could hear you breathe.
The time when you stood beside me,
And my skin glowed underneath.
The moment our eyes met, and we smiled,
I felt as if my heart was covered in flower wreaths.

You are the end of my sufferings,
You are the comfort when my heart's aching.
I only pray to the Lord to end this longing.
Hold me in your arms for once, to put me on end.
Let me shower you with all I have—
so that I'm left with no more love to spend.
I need you to put my heart on the mend.
Unveil my layers and rip my skin to shreds.

End me while I'm still breathing,
Leave me with nothing before leaving.
It's hard to breathe when my heart's still paining,
It's better to let me end myself with your hands,
Than yearning till my heart's beating.

12. Why So Pretty?

Why are you so pretty that it hurts?

Why are you so pretty that it makes my heart ache?

Why are you so pretty that it breaks my heart?

Why are you so pretty that it drives me nuts?

Why are you so pretty that you fix my heart without a word?

Why are you so pretty that I can think of no one else but you?

Why are you so pretty that it makes me fall in love?

Why are you so pretty that it makes me cry?

Why are you so pretty that it makes me smile, smile, and smile?

Maybe it's because it's all in my head,

Maybe you're not as pretty as I have said.

Maybe you're not pretty but beautiful,

That's why you make my dull life colourful.

Maybe the heart doesn't need a reason, it loves whoever it does.

Maybe I can say it as everybody does,

Or I should keep denying that it isn't love?

But the heart loves whoever it does,

And it knows if it is not or if it is love…

13. Love & Power

You, my love, are my power.
They say love weakens, but you make me feel empowered.
You make me feel dangerous—
when I have you behind me,
Even snakes aren't so poisonous—
When you are beside me.
You make me rather lethal than a coward.
You, my love, are my power.
You spoil me with your smiles—
When I stand up for myself.
Written on you I have poems' piles,
When I couldn't write one about myself.
I am parched and you're mid-August shower,
You, my love, are my power…

14. What is it?

You wonder what I like about you?
But what is it that I don't like about you?
When you shrug your shoulders like you don't care.
When you nod at everything I say, like you're always there.
When you move like the flowing water of a holy river.
Your smile makes my world light up my dear.
You wonder what I like about you?
But what is it that I don't like about you?

When you are so drowned in yourself, you don't hear anything.
When you get so comfortable you talk about everything.
When you act like a 'know-it-all.'
When you answer my call.
You wonder what I like about you?
But what is it that I don't like about you?

I like everything from when you breathe,
to when you sneeze.
From when you yawn to
Your radiant smile, like the break of dawn.
From your fingers gliding over your keyboard,
To your rolled-up sleeves.

You rip my heart like a sword,
Yet you're the cure to all my griefs.
You wonder what I like about you?
But what is it that I don't like about you?

15. Don't You Think…

Don't think that I don't love you because I look away,
I look at you when you're at a distance,
But can't look at you when you're close,
If I do, the world around me would fade away.

Don't think that I don't love you because I don't say it,
I don't say it but my eyes do.
Don't think that I don't care for you,
I hear things you don't say—
but your worn-out face does.

Don't think that I don't miss you,
I spend my days thinking about you,
Talking to the moon about you.
Don't think it was all a game,
I can't think of anyone the way I do for you.
Don't think that I don't love you,
I love you more than I thought I could love you…

16. Maybe in Some Other World

Maybe in some other world, you loved me too,
The way I do.
Maybe in some other world, I made your heart race,
The way you do.
Maybe in some other world, you prayed for the best for me too,
The way I do.
Maybe in some other world, my smile would take away your
gloom too,
The way yours does.
Maybe in some other world, you yearned for me too,
The way I do.
Maybe in some other world, I broke your heart a hundred times
too,
The way you do.
Maybe in some other world, I was snatched away from you too,
The way you have been.

But maybe in some other world,
I wish we could love each other at the same time.
Maybe in some other world,

I could call you mine.
Maybe in some other world,
I could see you beside me each night I dine.
Maybe in some other world,
We could see the stars shine.
Maybe in some other world,
Things would turn out just fine.
Well, maybe not in this world,
But maybe in some other world.
Maybe… in some other world.

17. Don't Be My Mother

Next time, if you get to live again,
Don't be my mother.
Wear tacky dresses with colourful feathers,
Dance through the nights, without any fear of the stormy
weather.
Be the girl you wanted to be,
Running along the seashore, climbing trees.
Live the ambitions you always had,
Colouring bright red, the blues, mundane and bland.
This time be the rebellious and mischievous child,
You always raised in me.
Drown in the extremes and don't touch the milds,
Be absurd and carefree.
Next time, if you get to live again,
Be selfish and mean,
And treat yourself the way you treat me.
Next time, if you get to live again,
Don't waste your time on me,
Explore mountains, and forests, and cross oceans and seas.
Be the water of flowing rivers,
Accept happiness, love, and laughter as much as you deliver.
Next time, if you get to live again,

Let your facade slide, and don't hide your reality,
Don't let the world mess with your sanity.
Because there's no second chance for second chances,
So next time, if you get to live again,
Choose yourself and not me,
Be anything you could be,
Let yourself this time be a Heather,
If you get to live again,
Don't be my mother.

18. Just A Man

Rocking in his armchair is an old man,
A man with lost hopes shattered dreams, and no clan.
We call him a father but forget he's just a man.
A man who had hopes and desires,
Gulping the warmth of youthful fires.
He sits here and tells me— "There's nothing that he has done,"
And yes he's right! Because toiling all day long isn't enough?
'Frayed shirts and worn-out shoes have a long way to go, they're
really tough.'
He couldn't be a good father, yeah that's right,
But he shows up at night with the favourite snacks of his child.
He doesn't know how to take care of himself,
Nor does he get to take some time for the books on that shelf.
No, he doesn't know how to be a father,
He's just a shattered man.
And he doesn't care if it gets harder,
Out of love for others, he can do everything he can.
He too must have had some dreams,
Like traveling the world and having the best coffee with extra
cream.
It's also his first time being a dad so be easy on him,

Because once he's gone, no one will turn on the lights when it's
dim.
I wish I could make him realise that I am proud of him,
Tell him that he's the reason I keep going,
When my eyes are filled to the brim.
Yeah, he's a father but also 'just a man,'
He too can make mistakes and change plans.
For the world, he's a father,
But to me, he's the most loving and sacrificing man.

19. Women In Love Are Crazy

Women in love are crazy,
A poisoned ivy, for you, is a daisy.
She does the most absurd things around you,
From acting like she owns you to making you feel understood too.
She acts like a 3 year-old kid around you,
She takes care of you like a mother too.
Give up all her warmth to you when it's hazy,
Women in love are crazy.

Looking at you when you are unaware,
Look away when your eyes meet theirs.
Smile at your very sight,
The thought of you in trouble gives them a fright.
When you say anything they are ready to fight,
And ready to fight the world for you and hold you tight.
Give up all their warmth when it's hazy,
Women in love are crazy.

Wants to tell you all the things going on in her head,
But when you're there—

she says everything but what she should have said.
She spends days planning how to get over you,
Right when she succeeds, she again falls for you.
Everytime someone asks she denies it,
But what other than love can one call it?
Give up all their warmth when it's hazy,
Women in love are crazy.
A poisoned ivy, for you, is a daisy.
Women in love are crazy.

20. The Little Things

There's nothing much I like about you,
But I like the little things that you do.
I like how you brush your hands through your hair.
I like how your eyes light up when you talk about something you
love.
I like your up-rolled sleeves.
I like the curve of your lips when You smile.
There's not much I like about you but there's nothing I don't like
about you…

21. The Torment of Love

Being away from you is the biggest torment.
Being with you is a torment too,
but a torment that I'd love to have.
The pain that makes me heal,
The agony that brings me joy.

Love always hurts and I chose it for myself and
I chose it for you.
I'd still love you if I was bleeding and my heart was ripping.
Yes! I'd love you with a ripping heart too.
Because loving you is a torment,
but not greater than the torment of being away from you.

22. Not My Mom

I looked at a picture and I could see my mom,
The way I smile, my glistening eyes,
It was not me but my mom.
The way I had kept my hands,
The way I laugh around my friends,
It was not me but my mom.
Those gentle manners and tender eyes,
That looking away when I get shy,
It's not me but my mom.
Loving heart and kind words,
Sometimes ordering around like I rule the world.
Sometimes valiant and bold, and sometimes a geeky nerd,
Free yet a caged bird.
It's not me but my mom.

But I don't want to be her!
I can't live with this choking fear,
Strangled by an invisible rope,
Pricked by thorns, a beautiful rose.
Always touched but never felt,
Dreams and desires shattered and crushed.
Fallen angel, scattered soul,

Bleeding all over, smelling foul.
I want to be cruel like this world,
I want to be valiant and not someone who's furled.
She's a delicate vine in a furious storm,
I wish I was 'her' but not my mom.

23. Another World

I hope to see you in another world,
Where your feelings will also be kindled,
Dancing on dimes with smiles pearled.
Where these 'made up' monsters will set me free,
Where I will run away from the spree of murdering me,
Where I will give you the best of me,
To deserve your love I'll have to cross this lifetime's sea.
I'll wait to meet you on the other side,
Where it'll be worth it, all the times that cried.
Dancing on the brink of the world kindled,
I hope to see you in another world,
Where all these demons won't be hurled,
I hope to see you in another world.

Where I'll breathe without choking,
Entwined in your arms, outside the window our love will be
snowing.
Where I won't be afraid of my own feelings,
When you look at me you'll start gleaming.
Where I'll live more than dreaming,
Where I won't be a mere sculpture only breathing.
Where I'll not dread the day you'd be leaving,

Where my own part's happiness I won't be stealing.
Where these wounds will stop reaming,
And my soul will no longer be bleeding.
Where I will also be worth loving,
Where destiny will end this yearning.
Running your hands through my hair curled,
I hope to see you in another world.
Didn't expect life the way it turned,
I hope to see you in another world.

Where my lungs will be filled with hope,
Not on this gagging smoke.
Where these murderous thoughts won't rip me,
Where these ringing in my ears won't wretch me.
Where I'll be 'enough,'
And I'll have you by my side if times get tough.
Where I'll stop bleeding off these cuts,
Where my heart will shovel off this rust.
Where I jump and still won't fall,
Where you'll answer each time I call.
Where the shards of my soul won't prick you,
And I'd be able to pick your shards too.
Where flowers would bloom right where it was burned,
I hope to see you in another world.
Before I thrust this twisted knife, I bid goodbye to the one I
loved,
I hope to see you in another world.

UMRA

24. Beyond The Seventh Sky

If I could even meet him beyond the seventh sky,
It'll be worth waiting a lifetime.
The sight of my love is the unguent to my wounds,
Fills my greys with vivid hues.
His silhouette is a blessing upon my soul,
Only he can quiet down my inner ghouls.
For even a glimpse of him, I suffer all the time's beating,
His soul has been planted in me, and now my love for him is
reaping.
I love my dear even harder as the spinning wheel rolls by,
He's all that I yearn for, he's what makes me cry.
If I could even meet him beyond the seventh sky,
It'll be worth waiting a lifetime.

I wouldn't say he ends my pain,
But he makes it more bearable.
I wouldn't say I love him in vain,
In this realm of stories, he's my favourite parable.
My being exalts beyond the skies,
When he is standing nearby.

In his soul all my peace lies,
Leaves my heart burning when he passes by.
For just a glance of him, I swim across the oceans and fly above
the skies,
He hums a song in my ears that I like.
If I could even meet him beyond the seventh sky,
It'll be worth waiting a lifetime.
I fear even touching him,
For my beloved is sacred.
I can't even look straight at him,
For my beloved is too bright for a soul that has faded.
Even his cast-off water can purify my blood,
He's the holy water and I'm a puddle of mud.
My heart yearns to dance to his paens on the streets,
Like a roadside vagrant, from the world who's free.
My soul yearns to lay under the soil he has walked on,
Such is my devotion and for him I long.
I don't expect anything so I won't even try,
But if I could even meet him beyond the seventh sky,
It'll be worth waiting a lifetime.

I've been so lucky to breathe the same air he breathes,
I beg for his happiness on my knees.
I've been so lucky to have my name on his tongue,
On his sleeves he has my heart strung.
He's the ease to my choked breaths,
He's the owner of the realm between my life and death.

He fixes my heart with his shy smiles,
He's named between my silent cries.
He's nature's sublime,
And my love beyond time.
Calling his name, on the bed of coals I lie,
If I could even meet him beyond the seventh sky,
It'll be worth waiting a lifetime.

25. Symphony Of Love

City lights light up by his smile,
He stands out even when he's away for miles.
My heart has a hollow space of his name,
Being with him is bigger than any fame.

He's all over my mind,
Can never believe my fate had been so kind.
Oh darling, how you can conquer the world with your smile,
With your name is painted my heart's every aisle.
Your scent follows me at every stand,
Your touch is carried in my hands.

When I talk about you, I run out of words,
Your voice is sweeter than any of those beautiful birds.
My darling! When you are mad at me,
I become as hopeless as I could be.
For you are even beautiful when you are mad,
But your broken heart makes me sad.

When my eyes meet the surface of your eyes,
I don't know what leaves them tied,
I can't seem to take them off you,

You have no idea how hard I have tried.
City lights light up with his smile,
He stands out even when he's away for miles.
His little eyes make me shine bright,
He's been tangled in my soul so tight.
His scent lingering under my breath,
Like a neatly intertwined flower wreath.
City lights light up by his bright eyes,
For him, and only him, my heart cries.

26. Loveliest Mortification

There's no bigger mortification than love, folks said.

But I couldn't help but love you.
I Loved you and God bestowed favours upon me,
for my sincere admiration for such a beautiful creation of his.

I loved you and beautiful things came to me—
in the most unexpected manners.
I loved you and smiled a little more.
You smiled and I loved you a little more.
There's no bigger mortification than love, folks said.
But I'd love you anyway!

27. Things I Want To Say

There are things I want to say to you,

But I'm scared you won't believe them to be true.

I want to tell you that I feel like hanging on a tree,

I want to tell you how these thoughts are killing me.

I want to tell you that I want to fly,

But my wings are clipped and I can only cry.

I want to tell you how this stab in my chest hurts,

There are things I want to say to you,

But when I try to speak, I can't find the words.

I can't tell you even if I try to,

So I keep writing poems on things I couldn't tell you.

Here lie all my secrets and the things I want to say to you.

Drowning in the air, buried under water,

I am slaughtered and I am the butcher.

I want to say to you, that your sight makes my skin breathe,

You're the drop of water in the scorching heat.

You're the knife that's got me ripping,

And yet keeps me from bleeding.

Writing suicide notes for the suicides I couldn't commit,

Quitting to live the life I couldn't quit.

There are unsent letters and unshared feelings too,

I couldn't say, so I write what I longed to tell you,
Here are knitted all the things I want to say to you,
The things I want to say to you…

28. I said I am strong, but I lied

I said I am strong, but I lied.
I was asked if I was fine and I smiled,
I struggled and yet I tried.
So I knit my words together and keep them tied.
I said I am strong, but I lied.

I gave my all when I wasn't full,
I radiated my light when my insides were dull.
I bled in front of a world so cruel,
My wobbly feet were still ready to fight.
I said I am strong, but I lied.

Though my days weren't bright,
I tried with all my might.
I dreamt of flying, though I was scared of heights.
I fell hard but no one could see my plight.
I said I am strong, but I lied.

I failed and no one told me that it was enough that I tried.
I looked around for help but found no one by my side.

UMRA

It was hard to breathe and harder to hide.
So I buried my face in a pillow and cried all night.
I said I am strong, but I lied.
I said I am strong, but I lied…

29. Why Not Me?

Why, why not me? I want to ask.
I gave it all up for you, unveiled myself without any mask,
Loved you like no other, when I knew from the beginning I had
no chance.
I pour myself into you and it leaves me all drained,
In love and shame, I'm all stained.
Why does fate have to be so harsh?
Why, Why not me? I want to ask.

I dreamed of being with you in your best and worst,
To be in every fold of your flaw sinking deep into your skin,
But now as I find the ashes of my heart burnt,
I stand here numb as the wheel spins,
It goes all back to how it was,
Why, Why always me? I want to ask.

You sleep like a bear and I watch you from afar,
I loved you to love myself and now I'm falling apart.
Your touch ignites a fire that burns my heart,
The way garlic bread tastes with a strawberry tart.
Maybe I never deserved you but it need not end before it even
starts,

UMRA

Why, why not me? Whom shall I ask?

Unleashing our souls shard by shard,
Sighing out in anguish in each other's arms.
Love does good but it can't keep you from harm,
People say that love comes back to you wherever you are,
But they forget some people can't be loved even if they try hard.
I was unfortunately one of those, so it's not your fault,
Each day I had to wage a war,
Only to realise I have gone too far.
But it hurts so bad to not even get a chance,
Why, why not me? Each day I ask.

The one that keeps me from breaking, breaks my heart,
Love is a dirty game but a beautiful art,
It makes the shattered fall apart.
To love someone I could never have and that too so hard,
It feels like I've been barred,
I still choose you anyway—
Now it makes me feel like a deuce in the game of cards.
Only you, that's all I ask,
Why, why not me? Will I ever get to ask?

Will I ever matter to you,
Even half as much as to me you do.
Will I ever be able to love someone the way I love you,
When I can't even look at someone the way I look at you.

I knew I never deserved you,
But why is it that when you talk to her like that, I can't stand
you?
Why do I burn while you dance under the spells she casts?
Why, why not me? That is all I want to ask.

If I can't have you then let me collapse in your arms,
Love to see you spellbound under her charms,
But why, why not me, is my right to ask.
I'll share your pearls and ugly laughs,
To love someone like you is an unbearable task,
But to not love you is too much to ask.
I burn for you and in your warmth, I bask,
Don't you think I deserved a fair chance?
Why, why not me? I want to ask.
Even if not me, just be happy,
Even if not me, you'd still be the only one I ask.
So even if not me just be happy, that is all I ask.

30. Gasping For Air

My love for you leaves me gasping for air.
All I wish is to have you near.
My worn-out soul wishes to collapse in your arms.
You got me on my knees with your charms.
My cursed skin wants to flourish under your sacred touch.
Other than you I don't ask for much.
Blessed are my eyes to have your sight, my dear.
My love for you leaves me gasping for air.
All I wish is to have you near.

31. All It Takes

If it takes for me to weep all night—
for you to be sound asleep then so be it.
If it takes for me to give my soul up—
for you to smile then so be it.
So be it, because I love to see you smile,
So be it, because I want to shower you with dimes.
So be it, because I love you after all,
So be it, because I can't let you fall.
So be it because I want to see you shine,
So be it, even if you can't be mine.
So be it, because you're spring in my fall,
So be it, because I'll be there if you call.
So be it, because I love you and it hurts,
So be it, and let me blurt.
If it takes for me to weep all night—
for you to be sound asleep then so be it.
If it takes for me to give my soul up—
for you to smile then so be it.
And if I can't do that all,
Then let me pray to my lord,
To keep you safe, because you have my heart out of all.

32. I Fear You

I love you, but I fear you.
I fear that if I pull away, I'll lose you,
I fear if I get too close, I'll lose myself.
I fear if I let you in you'd hate me too,
I fear if I let you go I'd hate myself.
I fear if you walk away it'll all turn blue,
I fear if I keep on holding I'd lose a hold on myself.
I fear if we fell apart I might never find someone new,
I fear I might stay stuck in this labyrinth.
I fear I'd regret things I never did,
I fear if I let loose, I'd fret over the things I did.
I fear that you might hate me,
I fear that you might not even remember me.
I fear that you'd never be mine,
What I fear more is I didn't try to be yours.
I fear that you'd never care for me,
I fear that you'd never know how much I cared for you.
I fear to appear foolish,
I fear being a coward.
I fear loving you,
I fear losing you.
I fear if I try to get a closer look, I might never come back.

I fear I'd never find someone better than you,
I fear I'd never be able to love someone the way I loved you.
I fear even if I tried to love someone else I'd wish them to be you,
I fear if you walk away, I'd lose myself too.
I fear that if I pull away, I'll lose you,
I fear if I get too close, I'll lose myself.
I fear if I let you in you'd hate me too,
I fear if I let you go I'd hate myself.
That's why I say that I love you but I fear you…

33. I Know This Is Foolish

I know this is foolish,
But for you my darling, I'd risk it.
Days will pass,
And we'll fall apart.
But no matter where we are,
You'll own my heart.
One day I'll walk away,
But "I shall forget you"– I beg you, do not say.
For you shall be the part of my supplications each time I pray.
I know I know this is foolish,
But for you my darling, I'd risk it.

Risk it because I am grateful,
And I shall persist in loving you though it's painful.
Risk it because you're not mine,
But I love those sparkles in your eyes.
Risk it because I love to make your cherry lips curl into a smile,
And I want to carry the memories that'll transcend time.
To make you the happiest creature in the world, my heart wishes,
I know this is foolish,

But for you my darling, I'd risk it.

You were never mine but I had always been yours,
To my heartaches, you seem to have all the cures
For you, all the pain my soul endures,
To you, I find my way back, as the ocean comes back to its
shores.
It's Unrequited the world might say,
But I can't help loving you—
For I was coarse and callous before you gave me your shade.
Your smile is the first thing I think of every day,
And I can't help loving you—
So I talk to my lord about you whenever I pray.
I know this is foolish,
But for you my darling, I'd risk it.

34. Anyway

I know that I'm stupid,
But I want you to love me anyway.
I know that I'm awkward,
But I want you to hold my hand in throngs anyway.
I know that I'm feeble,
But I want you to lean on me anyway.
I know that I'm scared,
But I want you to hold me anyway.
I know that I'm cantankerous,
But I want you to smile at me anyway.
I know that I can be cold sometimes,
But I want you to hear me anyway.
I know that I'm a nervous wreck,
But I want you to test your nerves on me anyway.
I know that I'm a cynic,
But I want you to trust me anyway.
I know that I'm bruised,
But I want you to consume my soul anyway.
I know that I'm ruined,
But I want you to ignite my heart anyway.
I know that I'm crazy,
But I want you to get into my head anyway.

I know that I'm stupid,
But I ask you to love me anyway.
I ask you to love me,
When I know that you can not.
I am stupid but I want you to tell me,
That "I'm not."
I know that you can not love me,
But I want you to prove me wrong, anyway…

35. The Way I Wanted To

Another woman will hold you, the way I wanted to.
Another woman will wipe your tears, the way I wanted to.
Another woman will tuck you in bed, the way I wanted to.
Another woman will bring you joy, the way I wanted to.
Another woman will hold your hand the way I wanted.
Another woman will kiss you good night, the way I wanted to.
Another woman will enjoy your coffee, the way I wanted to.
Another woman will read to you, the way I wanted to.
Another woman will start her day with your sight, the way I
wanted to.
Another woman will soothe your nerves, the way I wanted to.

But would she be able to love you as I do?
Would she choose you even if she knew you couldn't be hers?
Would the rainfall make her feel that you are seeping into her
soul?
Would the glowing sun remind her of your smile?
Would she be ready to plant a little part of her soul in you?
Would she spend aeons writing about you?
Would her blood turn gold just by sitting next to you?
Would she try to find every possible way to get to you?
Would she think about you when she sees the moon?

Would she want to be me, as much I want to be her—
If I was her, the way I wanted to?
Would she be able to love you as I do?

36. I Suffer Along

You think that when you suffer, you suffer alone.
But my love! When you suffer, I suffer along.
When you are hurt, I feel pangs of sorrow,
When you're sick, all of your ailments I want to borrow.
When you are mad, my heart burns with you,
When you're sad, my soul cries too.
When your heart aches, I feel the pain too,
When I close my eyes all I see is you.
You think that when you suffer, you suffer alone.
But my love! When you suffer, I suffer along.

I shudder at the thought of you being hurt,
To keep you spotless, I jump into heaps of dirt.
You're a drug and I'm overdosed,
When you're away, you're alright, that's all my heart hopes.
When you endure a loss, I lose something too,
When you suffer, I suffer with you too.
You think that when you suffer, you suffer alone.
But my love! When you suffer, I suffer along.

37. The Angel And Sinner

3 A.M. I am looking at your picture,
White string in the dark world—
An Angel to the eyes of a sinner.
Wine of love, taste of life,
That honey of your eyes intoxicates.
Sliding down my throat you burn it along the way,
Those lips with that smile, and my heart derailed.
Vehement preacher of those eyes—
When they are on me, my insides simmer.
My eyes, downcast when you're around—
Afraid to stain your ivories by the eyes of a sinner.

Everything beneath your skin is a holy grail,
Colours and scents of hope in the life of frails.
Oh, darling! Wherever you touched glows in the dark of the
night,
And ever since your eyes inspected that soul of mine,
It's been painted all over in the colours of life.
Demons keeping me up all night,
Strangling to the thread of hope, writing because I can not pull
the trigger,
3 A.M. I am looking at your picture,

White string in the dark world—
An Angel to the eyes of a sinner.
Neophyte poet couldn't write you better,
All I can say is– an Angel you are the eyes of sinners.
Under your gaze the withered bloom and sombre glimmer,
An Angel to the eyes of a sinner.
An Angel to the eyes of a sinner…

38. Where I went wrong?

I tried all the ways and gave it my all,
Still trying to figure out where I went wrong.
Piles of diamonds and jewels for them all,
Not even a penny for me, just a little dagger that prongs.
I've spent all my life trying,
Wrapped in a shroud are my dreams that I'm burying.
I'm always trying so hard,
But hatched nothing at all.
Never a victory but always a close call,
No one to grab me whenever I fall,
Still trying to figure out where I went wrong.

I have doubts and double thoughts,
A battle with myself and each day I fought.
Drowning, choking, and losing it all,
Once a loser is always a loser after all.
I'm all the way back to the start,
I feel stuck in a puddle like a wheel of a cart.
I want to give it up, but I can't,
No one to hold onto and nowhere to start.
I bleed each day, each night I fall,
Always an angel, never a god,

Still trying to figure out where I went wrong.

My breaths are choked and my mind blocked,
My luck is caged and the dreams padlocked.
I can't take my breaking heart and soul breaking apart,
All I've become is a ripped piece of art.
These desires strangle me, too overwhelmed to breathe,
My fibres burn and insides seeth.
'Good for nothing,' and it's been killing me,
Worked for dimes and can't even get pennies,
I'm dying and this shame is killing me.
Just wanna live once before I can't,
Still trying to figure out where I went wrong,
What was my fault?

39. When I'm With You

I lose track of time when I'm with you,
It's just me and you when I'm with you.
I lose my mind when I'm with you,
Just want to hear you talk when I'm with you.
When I'm with you, my worries are all gone,
When I'm with you, I feel for you I was born.
When I'm with you my soul smiles,
When I'm with you all my poems seem to rhyme.

Our energies mingle when I'm with you,
Weaving a symphony only we can hear.
My soul quivers when I'm with you,
Apart from you, nothing is clear,
When I'm with you.
When I'm with you I can't look at you,
Because if I do,
I wouldn't be able to look away from you.

The fibres of my body tremble in ecstasy when I'm with you.
I shiver when I try to show how much I love you,
And yet I can't help but express my love when I'm with you.
I want to yell and tell the world that I am in love with you.

*Moreover, I want to tell you that I love myself more when I'm
with you.
Thus, my darling, for an eternity I want to be with you.
Because I lose track of time with you,
It's just me and you when I'm with you.
Thus, my love, for the rest of my life I want to be with you.*

40. When it comes to you

Why is it so hard for us to forgive ourselves?
You forgave those who wronged you.
You forgave those who hurt you,
But why can't you forgive yourself?
You comfort others.
You support others,
But why can't you empathise yourself?

Why does it become so hard when it comes to you?
Challenges are not your problem,
your problem is you yourself.
Don't blame yourself.
Don't leave yourself astray.
Be there for yourself.
Don't push yourself away.
You need yourself more than anyone does.
You need yourself before you need anyone.

41. Fond of Paths

Somewhere on our journeys, we crossed paths.
I fell for the one I stumbled upon, and my beloved was fond of
the paths...

42. Fond of Travelling

I see you're fond of travelling my love,
but let me tell you my darling—
that once you're done you'll have a home in me to come back to.
My arms will be ready to hold you if you fall,
and my fingers…always ready to heal your wounds.

Oh bearer of my heart!
Just know that you can let your weary soul crash in mine.
Just know that you can take away my bloom,
to fill the chambers of your heart with my scent.
Just know you can fill your cracks with my melting heart.
Just know that you can make use of me till you find yourself.
Just know that my eyes will always be longing to see you.
Just know that even if you don't come back,
I'd still have your name imprinted on my heart.

I see you're fond of travelling my love,
but don't make my arms wait for too long.
You're my home and I have nowhere to go back to.
I see you're fond of travelling my love…

43. The Death of Youth Spring

Soon in the chaos of crowds,
You'll be out of my sight.
Soon I'll wrap my love in shrouds,
And bury it somewhere deep inside.

Soon my head will be filled with voices,
And your voice would fade away in the loud noises.
Soon I'll get used to being without you,
Soon I'll start believing that I got over you.

But when these noises will start fading,
And the mist of the crowds will start settling.
The moment when I'll become me again,
A little moment of peace again.
I'll look within myself just to find out that we were never apart,
You settle right there in the middle of my heart.
It was my dumb luck to have known you,
And most of me is now composed of some of you.

Soon I'll be away from you,

And soon I'll gather myself too.
But in any case my dear I'll never forget you,
Because if I try to forget you,
I'll forget myself too.
Soon I'll be left with moist eyes like the evening dew,
But shattering for something as beautiful as you had been worth
it too.

Soon I'll be away from you,
But I'll never regret losing you.
For I never deserved to hold a person as lovely as you,
My darling you're the greatest person I've met,
And you made me a great person too.
Though I couldn't have you,
I still feel grateful that God chose me to love you.
Soon I'll learn everything without you,
Learn everything but to forget you.

44. You Have Lost Me

I loved you with every part of me,
And one day you'll realise that you have lost me.
I loved you for nothing,
To bring to your life something.
But again I was left empty-handed,
Again I am left here stranded.
I loved you like no one ever loved me,
And one day you'll realise that you have lost me.

My heart would find ease with your sight,
And some days you'd become the reason for my plight.
I trust you with all my heart,
But I am sceptical of some of your parts.
Somedays you are the only one I think of,
Somedays you are the one I want to get rid of.
I loved you more than I could ever love me,
And one day you'll realise you have lost me.

Everyone I looked up to was snatched away from me,
Everyone I needed to be there, left me.
It's hard to decide if I should hang in there,
Or leave, knowing that you would never care.

UMRA

I feel grateful for your being there,
But there were times I thought I was something you couldn't
bear.
I come back again to where everyone had left me,
I still struggle to breathe,
A pitch-dark tunnel and a way out is something I can't see.
Loved to pieces though knowing that no one ever loved me,
I lost everything and you have lost me.

45. Love! Love?

People see the smiles,

And think love is a walk over flowerbeds,

But it's like walking on coals aimlessly for miles,

Loving is being in debt,

One repays all his life.

They think it's losing senses,

But it's when you're most sensible,

And yet you choose the things which make people say—

You must've lost your senses.

You secretly are capable,

"I love you," you still choose not to say,

You might lose them forever, you are afraid.

Love is a walk over flowerbeds,

But it's like walking on coals aimlessly for miles,

Loving is being in debt,

One repays all his life.

Stone on the lovers it pelts,

It burns so deep that their bones melt.

It feels like a knife thrusted in your heart,

It's like your soul ripping apart.

UMRA

It's a poison that turns you blue,
But your scarlet cheeks cover it for you.
And yet they smile,
As if it's a walk over flowerbeds,
While they walk on coals aimlessly for another mile,
Being in their beloved's debt,
That they repay all their life.

46. Genocide of Souls

Have you ever felt like crying, but no tears came out?
Expressing, but no words came out?
Wishing someone would notice, but no one did?
Internally screaming, but no one heard it?
Your eyes filled with pain but no one ever saw?
Living, but not actually living?
Feeling too much and feeling nothing at all?

It makes me think that either,
We are dead or the entire human race is dead.
We sit here waiting for someone to free our souls trapped in our
bodies.
And here are people out there
with dead souls, no love, compassion and empathy.
And we keep crying for help, to free ourselves in order to save the
human race,
And end this—
"Genocide of Souls."

47. My Parents Get Younger

Once a steady walker, now jerks as he moves along.
Once strong shoulders are now dropping on.
Once who wiped my tears, now cries hard,
The way I once cried over broken toys,
he cries when he loses the people closest to his heart.
He never said things going on with him, but now his silences are
longer.
It is now that I realise as I get older, my dad gets younger.

Once whom I tailed around, asks me to accompany her.
Once the one who treated my wounds, tells me "My hand is
aching my dear."
She can spot me from afar, though her vision is now a little
unclear.
It is now that I realised as I get older my mom gets younger.

They never stick around,
They talk about the whole town.
They want their way in everything,
Just like a three-year-old, stubborn kid.

They gave me warmth when days were colder,
In a blink I found myself grown up above their shoulders.
As I got older my parents got younger.
As I got older my parents got younger.

48. Get over it?

People say that you will get over it,
But is it possible when the love is true?
Is it not disrespect of your own self,
To claim to love them, and leave when it got rough?

Some say love leaves you astray,
Some say love is the only way.
Some say if love is true,
It will come back to you.
Well… it's been different for me,
For I found love only in its tragedies.
Somedays I feel like I am getting a hold of me,
Somedays I am just losing my sanity.

People say that you will get over it,
But those who say it, haven't tried being in love with him.
They haven't seen his charming smiles,
And his childlike eyes.
They don't know how well he is knitted with my shadow,
How I see him everywhere I go.
How I hate it when I see someone wearing his kind of shirt,
How when he says my name, feels like a kind of flirt.

I can look away, but his scent follows me,
I can run away but his memories chase me.
I surround myself with people and yet feel empty,
With joy everywhere around, I am always half happy.

Loving or leaving which one has more gain,
Whichever way, you'll lose something—
So I've learned to live with pain,
Off I go to become nothing.

People say that you will get over it,
But is it possible when the love is true?
Is it not disrespect of your own self,
To claim to love them, and leave when it got rough?

I hear him speaking through others,
It feels like a sin to be talking to another.
It burns my heart to ashes,
I run away and back to him, and it crashes.

People say that you will get over it,
But is it possible when the love is true?
Is it not disrespect of your own self,
To claim to love them, and leave when it got rough?

49. That one girl

That one girl, who smiles a lot.
That one girl, who cries over trivial things.
That one girl who is scared to lose the people she loves.
That one girl who panics around people.
That one who's loved yet lonely.
That one girl who gives her all but she's inwardly empty.
That one girl, who is boring but actually fun.
That one girl who doesn't think she's pretty.
That one girl who loves herself but sometimes hates herself too.
To that one lovely girl, don't doubt yourself,
You're not a human, you're a character straight out of a novel!
You're a rare dream that not all eyes are fortunate enough to see.

50. How'd You Know?

You say it must be easy for you.
But how'd you know, when you haven't even been me?
You haven't felt your brain getting numb to the spiral of your
thoughts.
You haven't felt your heart sinking to the ground.
You haven't felt the pressure pressing upon your shoulders.
You haven't seen all your gruesome memories dancing in front of
you.
You haven't felt thorns pricking in your throat.

I act cool, is what you can see,
but you won't see me raining like the first day of August.
You won't see me trembling to the level I could no longer stand.
You won't see me trying and trying but never being enough.

All you see is what I show you
and you say it must be easy for you.
But how'd you know, when you haven't even tried being me?
It's always easier to say than to sail in the same boat as me.
So there you tell me, it must be easy for you,
When you haven't even been me.

51. The Monsters of Head

She lay in her bed, the monsters had broken out.
She tried to quiet them but they were too loud.
She closed her eyes and they danced before her.
She gasped but there wasn't enough air.

With the monsters in her head, she lay in her bed.
She wondered if it would've been easier if she could express
herself better.
Would she be accepted, if she appeared a little happier?
Would she be loved, if she was a little popular?
The more she thought her heart got heavier.
So she lay in her bed, with monsters in her head...

52. Never Enough

I smiled through all the rough,
Little did I know that I could never be enough.
Sleepless nights, my body so cold,
And no one to call my own.
My head is always filled with noise,
Nothing to heal my heart's void.
Happiness was never meant for someone like me,
Love for me was far more than a luxury.
I loved more than I could give,
Still, my share is left empty.
Kept myself intact when times were tough,
Little did I know I could never be enough.

No matter, how hard I tried—
I was second to everyone.
And at times when I cried—
To wipe off my tears, I had no one.
Sometimes I can be a madwoman,
All I need is someone to understand,
Even if it's just one person,
Don't need something grand,
All I need is someone who'll understand.

UMRA

In pieces, I find myself,
trying to pull myself together.
Under the weight of my own judgement, I drown myself,
Everywhere I look, I find myself inferior to the other.
Nobody knows my fears
None of them has the count of my tears.
I smiled through all the rough,
Little did I know that I could never be enough.
Kept myself intact when times were tough,
Little did I know I could never be enough.

53. Implications Of Love

How do I tell you the implication of my love my dear,
My soul quivers when you're near.
Without your touch my soul sears,
The one that's ripping and yet keeping from bleeding, you are
that spear.
To be parted from you is my biggest fear,
Everything's blurred, only your sight is clear.
How do I tell you the implication of my love my dear,
My only wish is to have you near.
How do I tell you the implications of my love, my dear,
My soul quivers when you're near.
You lessen all the pain I bear,
You linger in my smiles and all of my tears.
You're the break of my dawn and my last dream of the night,
You painted the sanguines of hatred in snow white.
If I had you by my side I'd have no fear,
How'd you know the implications of my love my dear,
My only wish is to have you near.

How do I tell you the implication of my love my dear,
My soul quivers when you're near.
I wish to hold you when thunderstorms strike,

And I'll stick with you when you feel stuck.
I want to wake up next to you,
Hear your silence and read your eyes too.
To hide you in my embrace,
When you're on your inner demons' chase.
To be locked in your arms and disappear,
How'd you know the implications of my love my dear,
My only wish is to have you near.

How do I tell you the implication of my love my dear,
My soul quivers when you're near.
To be your morning coffee, and your late night's favourite read,
You weave a mystic song each time you breathe.
To walk hand in hand with in life's every mile,
To be the cause of your smile in your hard times.
Such are your little lover's desires,
To be a cool gush when your life's set on fire.
To witness your happiest of smiles and all the delights,
To be the only one you lose for and the only one you fight.
To see you happy and happier,
How'd you know the implications of my love my dear,
My only wish is to have you near.

How do I tell you the implication of my love my dear,
My soul quivers when you're near.
I spend my days in your memories and nights dreaming,
To be in the same frame with you in life's framing.

All I want is you against the world,
When I write about you, I lose track of words.
I've got a lot to say but I'm not good at expressing my dear,
How'd you know the implications of my love my dear,
My only wish is to have you near.
Your distance on me is severe,
All I wish is to have you near.
How'd you know the implications of my love my dear,
My love for you has made me bolder and yet it's the thing I fear.
How'd you know the implications of my love my dear?
How'd you know the implications of my love my dear…

54. Why Do My Dreams, Remain Dreams?

Why do my dreams remain dreams?
I see everyone getting their dreams come true,
While I wait for my turn in the queue.
They get even the wrong things they choose,
But when I love, I lose.
I am lost in the throng of people,
Can't take risks because I'll call for trouble.
I see them doing the things I wish I could,
Making me hate myself because if I wanted to, I would.
I'm stuck in this vicious cycle of life,
Where I want to live and then it seems like a crime.
I think I find solace in grief,
But then I want to be happy even if it's brief.
There are days when I'm not enough to love myself,
But all I have is me to heal myself.
I never had someone to call my own,
No one to jump into the water for me, while I drown.
My heart burns and my soul yearns,
You're on your own, that's what I need to learn.
No shoulder to cry on,

Hopeless I was born.
I'm still trying hard,
Telling myself I have to cross just a few yards.
No one to understand nor to hear,
Alone I had all this to bear.
Again I came to the start,
I make myself a fiasco, not an art.
This feeling is nothing new,
I see everyone getting their dreams come true.
While my dreams stay bound to my sleeps,
Why do my dreams remain dreams?

55. All I See

Every single thing around me reminds me of you,
Swerving waves in my heart, painting my heart blue.
Settled on my lashes large pearls of dew,
When I close my eyes all I see is you.

Why does my heartburn,
Why does it come back to you, even if you turn?
Why do I get painted in red and pink hues,
When I see you,
And then I find my heart broken into two.
Every single thing around me reminds me of you,
Swerving waves in my heart, painting my heart blue.
Settled on my lashes large pearls of dew,
When I close my eyes all I see is you.

Sometimes you make me smile,
Yet you also make me cry,
Loving you is aimless,
Your memories leave me breathless,
And I can't take it anymore,
But when I try to move on, I fall for you even more.
Every single thing around me reminds me of you,

Swerving waves in my heart, painting my heart blue.
Settled on my lashes large pearls of dew,
When I close my eyes all I see is you.

Loving someone when you don't stand a chance
That is maybe the hardest part.
I have learned to laugh without you,
But that laugh is not the same as it is when I'm with you.
Every single thing around me reminds me of you,
Swerving waves in my heart, painting my heart blue.
Settled on my lashes large pearls of dew,
When I close my eyes all I see is you.

56. The Little Girl

There lived a little girl with dreams and desires,
She spent her days aiming to get higher.
Her world was very small and merry,
She thought the world worked like those of fairies.

Her world was shattered at a very young age,
Her little world had now become a cage.
Her lively summers were now filled with chilly haze.
Her heroes failed her,
Her most trusted betrayed her.

Then someone held her hand for a short while,
And let her lean on him to walk for a mile.
The abandoned girl found comfort in his soul,
Thus falling in love with him beyond control.
Her scorched soul found comfort in his cold heart,
But fate didn't take too long to make their ways apart.

The abandoned girl lost the one she could never call her own.
She still kept wandering in the hope of finding an actual home.
Her dreams and desires,
Were turned to ashes after fire.

For everyone who was her beloved,
Left her trust crushed.
There was only person she wanted to stay,
That last salvager, who was also brutally snatched away.

He would still be her beloved,
His smile was the thing she most cherished.
For even a while, he made her smile,
And helped her to make it to another mile.
Her dreams and desires,
Were turned to ashes after fire.
She lay bloodied on the battlefield,
Still aiming to get higher.

57. Thanks For Breaking My Heart

Thanks for breaking my heart,
Thanks for leaving me when I was falling apart.
Thanks for reminding me that love for people like me is more
than a luxury,
A vagrant like me couldn't own that treasury.
Thanks for breaking my heart,
Thanks for leaving me when I was falling apart.

Again I bleed and no one's here to hold me,
Again I traded my love for free.
Again my own weight is drowning me,
Again my heart is left empty.

Thanks for breaking my heart,
Thanks for leaving me when I was falling apart.
Thanks for reminding me,
No one loves those who can't love themselves.
No one loves those who need it the most.
Thanks for breaking my heart.
Thanks for leaving me when I was falling apart.

• 106 •

58. You'll Never Know

You will never know what I go through,
I'll laugh like a maniac though my insides are bruised,
You will never know what I go through.
You see whatever I make you,
Still, I know I can never be like you.
I can never get the things I want,
A struggle for me, for you is a jaunt.
Throngs leave me feeling empty,
While I watch them with their bags filled aplenty.
Yet you'll never find out how my life is screwed,
You will never know what I go through.

Each day is a battle with myself,
You would never know how I had put up with the roughs,
Knowing that I would still not be enough.
I laugh through it all but you won't see how my insides hurt,
You won't see me smeared with blood and dirt.
You won't see me when I'm a crying mess,
I know if I let you in, "I'll be just making a fuss."
Each day my silent sobs strangle me to death,
Every moment makes it harder to draw in a breath.
I'm all painted in grey and blue,

But you'll never know what I go through.

I'm scared of falling,
But you won't see me backing off darling.
I see people having each other's backs,
But when I need someone 'I'm just a crack.'
No one is there for me, that's something I have learned,
As I see the world watching me burn.
You can laugh because you have never been there,
Go ahead and mock me, I don't care.
Your jokes make me laugh,
But it hurts in my chest where I have a stab carved.
I'm torn to shreds, yet no one knows,
I wish to end this dream with my eyes closed.
You don't even know half of my agony from what I show you,
Thus, you'll never know what I go through.

I wish I had someone to lean on too,
I wish someone would hear me too.
Each day I wish I was someone new,
Each day I wish I was more like you.
I wish I had someone to understand me,
Whereas even I end up making myself feel lonely.
Each day my excitement for this foul world dies away,
Still, I fight to keep going every day.
If I had to die today, I'd be fine,
But before I meet that time,

I just want to live once, before I die.
My battles our way different than you,
Thus, you'll never know what I go through.
You'll never know what I go through.

59. Dervish Of Love

Tormented by the world, Dervish of love.
Star crossed, crossed paths,
A knife thrusting right into my heart.
Two burning flames and seething start,
One burns everything he looks at,
One got its eye on the other and is now falling apart.
One is the morning's glow, the other is a dreary dove,
Painted in golds of love and chained by the world,
Timeless is love but time's always in a rush.
Tormented by the world, Dervish of love.
When the eyes meet in bustling bazaars,
The soul transcends time, what are minutes and hours?
My soul doesn't have a rhythm of its own,
No song and the heart is forlorn,
It dances at the beloved's heartbeats, in his breaths it drowns.
I'll get him the reds of roses and take all the pricking thorns,
He's the morning glow and I am the dreary dove.
Tormented by the world, Dervish of love.

You come to realise that only you were feeling this way,
The heart buried under the weight of the things you couldn't say.
The moments slip away,

The soul was stranded and the heart disarrayed.
Tongues of fire engulf my soul, and the smoke and mirrors take
him away.
Love is ugly yet I chose to stay,
Trade my tears for his happiness all night and day,
Ripping, screaming, bleeding, I lay.
Because he's the morning glow and I'm the dreary dove,
Tormented by the world, Dervish of love.
Dancing, singing, and drifting away from the world,
Flying in reverie is this dreary dove.
Tormented by the world, Dervish of love.

60. Fool For Love

They say things and leave me strained,
Breaking through my heart's rift, blood all drained.
Walking on the glass pieces,
I hear your name and my heart ceases.
Blazing wounds under my skin,
My heart is full of you to the brim.
Frozen bones, tears of blood,
Drained of the blood, skin covered with mud.
Numb to the core,
My heart is aflame and soul forlorn.
Floating underwater,
My dreams and hopes are getting slaughtered.
The river has turned red, killed by small grits,
Falling back into grief's dark pit.
They say things and laugh at me,
But what can I say?
Fool for your love, can't set myself free.
I tried to be your shade just like a tree,
Now like little kids here, you and her play,
I burnt under the scorching heat, but you never thought of me.
You pull my strings and twist my heart,
Like a house of cards, I fall apart.

I'm sick and tired, get me over with my part,
When you look at her with soft eyes it burns my heart,
And when she touches you, it leaves a burning mark.
They say things and leave me strained,
Breaking through my heart's rift, blood all drained.
They laugh at how your love has my neck chained,
But no one can see my soul strangled.
They say things and leave me strained,
Falling through my heart's rift, blood all drained.
Bleeding feet, your floor stained,
You have no idea how much these unfortunate eyes have rained.
They say things and leave me strained,
Falling through my heart's rift, blood all drained.

61. Turn Into Soil

Turn into soil oh children!
Who's the great hero and who's the villain?
They're all the same for the soil,
So turn into soil oh children!
Share your plate with others and double you shall be given,
Let your sins be spoilt,
For soil doesn't care if you have a penny or a million.
So turn into soil oh children!

Why do you care about the colour and the caste?
When from the same soil all of you 'He' casts?
Not very long are your beauty and pride going to last,
Time turns the tables surprisingly fast,
So choose what you lose and what you gain.
Break it into half even if you have one grain,
It's all from the soil,
So turn into soil oh children!

Let flowers bloom through you,
And let the waters flow.
Mould yourself however you want to,
And burn in the glaze so that you may glow.

Resist the flames of magnitude,
So that with rising smoke you may rise and grow.
In the worldly chaos and turmoil,
Nothing is as tranquil as soil.
So turn into soil oh children!

And don't be barren and crude,
For that'll bring you neither flowers nor fruits.
Sow generosity and reap love,
And you shall be placed heaven above.
Laugh with kids rich or poor,
Lest their innocence be stolen by the cruels.
Destiny bows for those, in the name of love who toil,
For giving is the nature of the soil.
So turn into soil oh children!

62. Never Again!

If I'd leave this time, you may never see me again.
If I lose my way this time, I may never find my way back to you
again.
A weight is pressing upon my heart,
It hurts like it was hit with a burning dart.
I am rising like grey fumes,
Misty and hazy; as my soul this fire consumes.
If I exhale, I may never breathe again.

Don't look away! Watch my heart burn in grief,
As your resentment devours me piece by piece.
Heap of mud with a void for the sake of soul,
Won't you breathe life into this purple ghoul?
Choking on fresh air, pricked by flowerbeds,
Strangled by life and dodged by death.
If I turn away this time, you may never see my face again.
If I turn my back this time, I may never look at you again.

Your longing is a slow poison, pulsing in my veins,
Drowning in this endless rift, engulfed in overwhelming
hurricanes.

*Mourning over the corpse of my love, I've turned as pale as
death,
With your voice ringing all over my head, my ears have turned
deaf.
If I walked away this time, you may never get to call my name
again.
If I kiss you goodbye, you may never wish me morning again.
Take your time and think again,
If you let go of this hand this time, it won't hold you again.*

63. He and I

He and I are so alike,
With those shy smiles and stubborn minds.
And when we try to make eachother laugh,
As if his soul was parted in two and I'm the other half.
We have our own parts to play,
But still, try to make it easier for each other every day.
He's the thread that lets me loose and makes me fly,
And I'm the kite he can make reach the seventh sky.
He and I are so alike,
With our shy smiles and stubborn minds.
He and I are so alike,
You can see it in our bright shining eyes.
The kind of faces we make,
And when we steal cherries from cakes.
I am a flowing river meeting his sea,
He is the wind swaying me like a tree.
Acting like a child,
And our love for the wild.
He and I are so alike
With our shy smiles and stubborn minds.
He and I are so alike,
He's the reason my poems rhyme.

I am the dust of his feet,
My heart chants his name with every beat.
He's the lightbulb for my fuse,
He puts this useless thing to use.
I'm the artist and he's my muse,
Among throngs of people, still him, I'll choose.
He's my first thought in the morning and the last dream of the
night,
My pain eases only by his sight.
He and I are so alike,
With our shy smiles and stubborn minds.
Bitter yet sweet kinds,
He and I are so alike,
With our shy smiles and stubborn minds.

64. The Home I long

These people, these customs don't amuse me anymore,

These chowks and bazaars, don't amuse me anymore,

This home and the people, I don't belong with anymore.

I long for the mountains you have your abode in,

I long for the river where you chant my name,

I long for the soil you belong to,

I long for you and your soul,

I long to run away from here and to be where you are,

I long to be where it's only us,

I long to be spellbound in your charms and drown in your arms,

I long for the long-abandoned soul turned vagrant in your love,

I long for the place I belong to and the home I love,

I long for my skin to rekindle under your touch,

I long for my soul to balter over the symphony of your breaths,

I long for the tears I couldn't cry anymore and the memories I

couldn't live anymore.

These people, these customs don't amuse me anymore,

These chowks and bazaars don't amuse me anymore,

This home and the people I don't belong with anymore.

I long for the long-abandoned soul turned vagrant in your love,

I long for the place I belong to and a home with you my love.

65. If I could be a child again

If I could be a child again,
I'd have been a little insane.
Sailing in oceans, crashing imagination's planes,
Showering in the midnight rain.
If I could live my life again,
I'd swing endlessly on swings of flames,
Child of earth setting water aflame.
Never knocking upon the failures and disdain,
If I could be a child again.
If I could live that life again,
Would've been the evening breeze than autumn's rain.
I'd dance my heart out to my heart's own rhythm—
Even forgetting my own name.
I'd burn myself in vicious brame,
Stand against every false statement and false claim.
Let that virtuous girl also bring some shame,
If I could be a child again.

If I could be a child,
This time I won't chase fame,

I'd try to be dangerously tame.
This time I'd not let love take the bait.
I'd not have any regrets or anyone to blame.
This time I'd be something more than a pawn—
Stomping on every piece of this game,
I'd be something more than a mere name.
Just a little child like a fatal fire and not flickering flame,
If I could be a child again.

If I could jump in puddles of valiance again,
I'd never clutch onto hopes so lame,
I'd simply wander and not settle in temporary crames.
Cradle myself in my arms and wouldn't run after aimless aims.
This time I'd also try to be a part of my family's photo frame.
If I could be a child again,
I'd try to live this time for my own sake,
If I could be a child again.
If I could be a child again…

66. Evening Of Dehradun

I am a bustling street of Delhi,
He's the breezy evening of Dehradun.
He's the bright sun of the skies,
I dance around him like the earth, ready for her doom.
His giggles ringing in my ears,
Are like golden flames dancing amidst glooms.
His scent can intoxicate the best of man,
He ties my breaths in tune.
His gaze can melt the unbreakable stones,
When he walks away I feel as if I'm floating in poisonous fumes.
I am a bustling street of Delhi,
He's the breezy evening of Dehradun.
He's the cozy blanket in colds,
His eyes unveil my soul till the last of folds.
We met each other on crossing roads,
Miles apart but close enough to hold.
He's like the first dance in every ballroom,
In the pitch dark, he rises like brume.
He's the cool breeze fluttering my hair at midnight in June.
He's the flower of life and I am the last nail of the tomb.
I am a bustling street of Delhi,
He's the breezy evening of Dehradun.

He's a perfectly brewed morning coffee,
I am that ordinary 'tapri wali' evening tea.
From peacocks, he has learned to flee,
And he has those eyes sparkling like waves of a sea.
One who's stitched my heart together, he's that loom,
Seeing the gold of his skin seethes even the moon.
I am a bustling street of Delhi,
He's the breezy evening of Dehradun.
I had jumped into flames, embracing my doom,
That's when his gentle breaths came to my rescue.
I am a bustling street of Delhi,
He's the breezy evening of Dehradun.
He's the breezy evening of Dehradun…

67. Pastry shop

A little girl of three,
In front of her favourite pastry shop beside the Banyan tree,
Staring at the last piece of her favourite pastry,
But in her pockets, she didn't even have a penny.
She looked at the shopkeeper with a glint of glee,
Asking the owner if she could have the pastry piece for free,
But the shopkeeper thundered at the little girl's bravery—
And told her, "That I'll hand this piece to only the one who's
worthy."
So, the little girl waited, and waited patiently,
But something else was written for her in this tragic parody,
Such was the consequence of her barbarity,
Another woman came and took it away—
She stood there shocked at the finality,
As she saw the woman having it gallantly.
She couldn't help but cry at the fate's brutality,
She looked for some other pastry pieces too—
But none of them was anything like her favourite pastry,
The kid wanted to throw a fit furiously,
But all she could do was accept it as destiny,
And never even look again at that 'Shop of Pastry.'

68. Moonchild

As the sun turns its back on Earth,
And the moon shows up sparkling silver dust.
You're the one who crosses my mind first,
No second, no third, only you last and you first.
Each day passes by with the hope of seeing you again,
I tell the moon every night how my love was all in vain.
I see your glimpse as you reflect through the silver glass,
Waiting by the stairs of hope, my days pass.
'Why is it so hard?' I ask the moon,
He smiles back at me and tells me it's not only you.
For he too sees the earth burning for the sun,
Yet tip-toes in to kiss her goodbye when it's in a complete lull.
I wait for the sky to melt and you fall into my arms,
My tarnished soul, ready to catch you and keep you from any
kind of harm.
Let this be the last night,
I don't want to keep this fight.
Let it be the end and don't let me see the next sun shine,
Even if the world ends tonight, we'll be fine.
Put your hand mine,
And let me melt in your arms so divine.
If I don't see the next sun shine,

But you hold me tight this night,
I'll be just fine.
Loving you makes me so sick, it almost feels like a crime,
What's a crime, I'll paint myself in sin, if you tell me that you're
mine.
Oh, my love! You're so pretty that you almost make me blind,
They say the moon gets its shine from the sun, but oh darling,
you make it shine.
I sit under the sky, as my world churns,
Cradling in dancing flames, my body all covered up with burns.
As the sun turns its back on Earth,
And the moon shows up sparkling silver dust.
You're the one who crosses my mind first,
No second, no third, only you last and you first.

69. Regret

I often regret the things I did not say,
Then I also regret the things I said.
It seems like regret is the only thing entwined in my soul,
I don't know what thoughts are mine.
What can I call my own?
I want to jump from cliffs,
I want to be bold,
Yet I fear slipping through the rifts,
Lying on the floor, dead and cold.
I regret letting the days slip away,
I regret every night's fray.
I regret the way I am,
I regret the person I sham.
I regret the person I should be,
I grieve the person I wanted to be.
I regret those hopeless cries,
I regret all those failed tries.
I regret smiling through the pain,
I regret trading everything off with no gain.
I regret the day that is to come,
I regret the person I've become.
Sometimes I regret it all,

The ruthless summer and vengeful fall.
Sometimes I regret some of the things,
Often I regret it all.

• 129 •

70. The Crime I Write

Like a crumpled paper, I hide my secrets between these lines,
Old and crinkled, I've grown before time.
I've come to unleash myself here and try to make it rhyme,
Cause there's something killing me and maybe I'm committing
this crime.
A hysteric mother and a broken father awaiting me at home,
I bury all my emotions inside my heart's tomb.
All I want is someone to hold me when things go wrong,
And a place where I belong.
Carrying the weight of being a 'good woman,' on my feeble
shoulders,
Bleeding and fighting, stumbling upon these boulders.
Can't speak or cry,
Soaked in scarlet here I lie.
Can't speak so I write,
Staining with my sins the prettiest of whites.
You can hear here my soul's shrieks,
You'll find here the most of me.
Can't remember which part of me is more true,
So I sit and think it through;
And blur the lines between reality and pages,
So that I might die and still live for ages.

I try but lose it when it gets tough,
Always last in the race of being 'enough.'
I am fearful and lost,
Lonely and petrified in the responsibilities' frost.
All I want is a shoulder to lean on when I get tired,
Some arms to flee to when I am scared.
I want to be understood,
To be loved irrespective of whether I am 'bad' or 'good.'
For once I don't want to be so brave,
For once, I want to be cared for even if I act naive.
For once, I want to be where nothing is expected,
And the whole of me is accepted.
To get lost in an unknown place,
Where my soul is entwined with someone in a third space.
To be able to connect,
And be someone who's also loved.
To be able to feel and be touched,
To break free of the chains that are cursed.
To be known for my worst,
And still not be considered as a curse.
All I want is to be loved and be respectable,
But I end up being the side character of my own fable.
So I sit and write things that aren't true,
And the things that aren't so untrue.
I write suicide notes of the suicides I had to commit,
And the love letters to the love I just couldn't forget.
Here in the casket are my strangled thoughts,

Mounting over this grave is my poems that rot,
Devouring it are the feelings of grief and loss,
Of unfulfilled dreams and a love long lost.
Like a crumpled paper, I hide my secrets between these lines,
Old and crinkled, I've grown before time.
I'll just bury another feeling and try to make it rhyme,
Cause there's something killing me and maybe I'm committing
this crime.

71. Do Not Weep Over The Bygones

Do not weep over the bygones.
Once it gets dark and you're all alone,
Do not weep over the bygones.
Do not weep over friendships that did perish,
For they gave you memories to cherish.
Do not weep over the people you've lost,
Do not weep over the memories— dead and frost.
It's a long way and you'll have to walk over thorns,
Do not weep over the bygones.

Do not weep over the good old days,
When you had snow fights in the chilly haze.
Do not weep over the days when everything was fine,
When you were dancing over heaps of dimes.
You may get that all back but your flesh and bones,
Do not weep over the bygones.

Do not weep over the grief of the lost,
For they once gave you delight when your paths crossed.
Do not weep because it's not the same,

To add to your life there'll be many more names.
Do not weep over once gems turned stones.
Do not weep over the bygones.

Do not weep over the dusty sky,
If the sun is wrapped in clouds,
That doesn't mean it's a lie.
Do not weep over the parch and dry,
The liveliness of life is wrapped in shrouds,
Doesn't mean you'll have to cry.
Put all the loveliest nosegays on its gravestone,
But do not weep over the bygones.
Do not weep over the bygones…

72. Dead and Gone

Every morning was a hope to get to you,

You painted in scarlet and gold all of my blues.

You were unction to my scars,

But now you're as far as the stars.

My lips don't remember how to smile,

Tears well up in my eyes.

My cries can't reach your ears,

Dark shadows dance in front of me, I am back to all my fears.

My veins carry the sensations of your longing,

My skin singes in agony when your memories prong me.

The trails of your touch make my wounds sear,

Oh! How can I ever forget you, my dear?

Every mundane Monday was a hope to get to you,

It settled over my parch leaves like the morning dew.

But now on my Mondays I just want to sleep in,

As it temporarily numbs my blazing skin.

I see your memories burn in the flames of my heart,

I still chose you, though I knew the ending from the start.

I bury you with my own hands,

In the last fold of the earth where the world ends.

My favourite face has now been veiled,

I would never see the only face I wished to see.

Now I have to let go,
But I am still waiting with the hope of seeing you tomorrow.
Though I know I can never have you back,
Your giggles still echo in my heart's cracks.
Your smiles dance in front of me,
It'll be the last day of my life when your memories will set me free.
Would be able to have you if there was a next life,
Or am I cursed to dig into the depths of plight?
I wish you had broken my heart,
So that I could forget you when we fell apart.
But here I am picking my wretched soul,
And the weight of your memories' ghoul.
I weep over the tomb of the memories of me and you,
I know that you're dead and gone but I can't let go of something as dear as you.

73. The Funeral

Traces of dried tears on her rosy cheeks,
Her strength all drained away, yet she pretended that she wasn't
one of the weaks.
A heavy blow at the early stage of her womanhood,
They wanted to ease her pain but no one could.
All of the colours drained away from the lovely blossom,
Under all the mourning and wailing voices, her brain was
numb.

A mother with skin sunken deep,
But her heart sank deeper.
Who always waited for her son so that she could eat,
Now waited for the inevitable so that they would again meet.
Her heart ripping out of grief,
Wished the agony to be as brief as it could be.

Far away in the corner sat a silent lady,
Her love was snatched away from her before she was even ready.
She ran her fingers over his face for the last time,
Tracing his face under her skin for her lifetime.

A young lad and his father's beloved son,

Now wanted to go back in time as fast as he could run.
The shoulders he dreamt to get patted on someday,
Were now carrying him, on what in his life was marked as the
"Black Day."
There were hundreds to back him up,
But none could give strength to his shaking hand,
when he covered his beloved father's grave with sand.

Death is agony or the agony is for the ones they leave behind?
Jealousy, hate, and ego, this world is a lie,
Death is the truth of life,
and my lord is the utter truth for mankind.

74. The End Call

Each day I wage a new war.
Some days it's a war with myself.
Some days it's a war between my mind and heart.
Some days it's a war in what I call "home,"
Some days it's a war for love.
And some days it's a war against the world.
But today I call it off.

It's my last war as your last warrior.
It's my last time being my numb soul's carrier.
I lie on the battlefield in a blood pool,
My wounds state stories of fate too cruel.
I immensely loved but was left empty-handed,
No one by my side I lie here stranded.
Loved till the end of the world,
Still couldn't conquer love.
After all the struggles my life still turned out to be a flop,
I fought every battle with a new hope, but today I call it off.

75. I Shall Be Gone

One day I shall be gone,
Endless sleep and mute songs,
Returning to the soil I belong,
No more voices and away from the throngs.
One day I shall be gone.
Humming life's lovely songs,
Returning to the soil I belong,
One day I shall be gone.

But before I die I want to live,
Whatever I was rewarded with,
I want to give.
Before life slips away,
I want to tighten my grip.
Drink through the sacred cup the waters of love,
So that I may die, but my soul shall survive.
When dusk will prevail—
And I won't be able to witness the dawn,
One day I shall be gone.
Returning to the soil, I belong,
One day I shall be gone.

Shrouded under the folds of the Earth,
Laying above inches of hearth.
What shall be the dimes and what shall be dirt?
When all the rich and poor shall be sharing the same berth.
The sanguines shall be blue and curt,
Those helpless shall no longer hurt.
Your people shall leave you without a frown,
One day we all shall be gone.
Returning to the soil where we all belong,
One day we all shall be gone.

But I want to make my voice count before it's unheard,
I want to be a little weird and absurd.
I want to love and be loved,
Before I'm forgotten I want to be remembered.
I want to breathe before my breaths are ceased,
Before I turn into a phantasm I want to be believed.
Want to be someone's, before I'll be no more,
So that I may die, but my love shall live on.
Returning to the soil, I belong,
One day I shall be gone.

76. When I'm am gone

When I am gone, think of me fondly,
And tell my tales to your children.
Water my garden, if my absence turns it barren.
When my door gets knocked on by a raven,
And Fate unravels the truth bitter and ugly,
Think of me fondly.

When I am gone, think of me fondly,
And let my smell waft through your home,
Let them hear me through your words, once I am gone.
When I return to where I belong,
When your children won't go to sleep, sing to them my favourite
songs,
Give me life through your house so lively,
When I'm gone, think of me fondly.

Think of me fondly,
And tell my tales to your children.
See me laugh through their laughs,
Find me in the warmth of your coffee in December.
Lest dust not sit on the pages of my stories,
Treasure me in your reminiscence, like a precious piece of Amber.

UMRA

Remember me when you smell nosegays as pretty,
When I'm gone, think of me fondly.

When we meet where the sky melts, after the end of an eternity,
Do not forget to embrace me and tell me,
That you did not forget to remember me,
Not every day, just once after a long spree.
And I'd tell you that you're still as lovely,
So, when I'm gone, think of me fondly,
And let my smell waft through your soul,
And tell my tales to everyone.

77. End of Beginning

The city has turned cold,
Hailing sky calls to break free from the mould.
Waving earth is drowning the sky,
Melting mirrors are waving goodbye.
Ousted from the city, who never knew me.
Save tears for the midnight,
Unknown though I was, I knew the city.
Though one last sunset in the city, my heart is yearning,
I look away and wave goodbye to the beginning.

Gone to an alien land, I will come back someday,
I preserve the fragments of these dead days,
And look for my traces in its hay-day.
I beg for another day,
Whatever the price I'll be ready to pay.
'Once out of the city, never back,' they say.
Thus on the outskirts of my beloved place, I'd like to stay.
I'll leave the place but my heart will never be leaving,
Turning my back, I wave goodbye to the beginning.

Abandoned by the city, not an abandoned man,
Quests for dust, separated from the clan.

Carrying the giggles of the loved ones in my head,
Those will be the only memories echoing before I'm dead.
The kingdom will burgeon with late autumn's rain,
Take me out of the city, and you'll still find me across the lane.
My home will breathe in me, even if I'm away from it,
Maybe it's time to wave goodbye to the beginning.

It's time for a battle at the world's bay,
Tearing and bleeding my soul is astray,
But I promise one day,
I'll find back my way.
Under the blazing sky, for a night I'll stay.
'It is all the same for me,' I'll say,
Though amidst unknown faces I'll know everything has changed,
But underneath my skin—
the dreams and the city will remain unchanged.
Under the fire-lit sky, I'll see it all ending,
I wave goodbye to the beginning.
Till the day I witness the beginning of the ending,
I say goodbye to the beginning.

78. Coffee Shop:

Let's get locked in a coffee shop,
And lose track of that clock on the wall.
You get me all my   favourite flowers,
And I drown in your eyes of the colour of chocolate tart.
You smell like croissants,
And drink coffee from my lip-stained spot.
Let's get locked in a coffee shop,
And lose track of that clock on the wall.

Stroke my hair before the coffee gets cold,
And let my dreams unfold,
Let's talk about the things you never told,
And look me in the eye and find what a sight you are to behold.
Snuggling in each other's arms at a frozen hilltop,
Let's get locked in a coffee shop,
And lose track of that clock on the wall.

Be as miserable in love as I am,
And I'll show you in your love, how many oceans I swam.
Even if that coffee is poisoned and it burns my heart,
It won't do me a thing if I have you to bogart.

Give you all the warmth like your morning coffee, and won't let
your tears slop,
Let's get locked in a coffee shop,
And lose track of that clock on the wall.
You smell like croissants,
And drink coffee from my lip-stained spot.
Let's get locked in a coffee shop,
And lose track of that clock on the wall.

Epilogue:

Here ends this book and a beautiful chapter. I hope my words made you feel the deepest of emotions that had been left untouched in the corner of your heart. These words belong to me but the feelings are all yours. Take these words with you and express yourself. The most human thing about us humans is– having a heart and expressing what it feels. Live the moments of your life. Good or bad, immerse yourself in them and feel them. Beauty is pleasing and beauty is terrifying, so immerse yourself in whatever you have. Leave no feelings repressed anymore. Come back here when you need to feel something and you'll find these words as fresh as if you had never known them before.

At last, I pay my heartiest gratitude to you for spending a part of your life reading my book. May you live a happy and fulfilling life.

Thank You!

www.ingramcontent.com/pod-product-compliance
Lightning Source LLC
Chambersburg PA
CBHW021206130726
47988CB00002B/533